FEED MY CHILDREN

I0617994

Joseph From Rags to Riches

WRITTEN BY
FLABIA THEMBEKA

INK START MEDIA
265 Eastchester Dr Ste 133 #102
High Point NC 27262

From the Series

The Bible Coming To Life In the Eyes Of The Children

TABLE OF CONTENTS

GENESIS 39-41 (KJV)

39And Joseph was brought down to Egypt; and Potiphar, an officer of Pharaoh, captain of the guard, an Egyptian, bought him of the hands of the Ishmeelites, which had brought him down thither.

²And the Lord was with Joseph, and he was a prosperous man; and he was in the house of his master the Egyptian.

³And his master saw that the Lord was with him, and that the Lord made all that he did to prosper in his hand.

⁴And Joseph found grace in his sight, and he served him: and he made him overseer over his house, and all that he had he put into his hand.

⁵And it came to pass from the time that he had made him overseer in his house, and over all that he had, that the Lord blessed the Egyptian's house for Joseph's sake; and the blessing of the Lord was upon all that he had in the house, and in the field.

⁶And he left all that he had in Joseph's hand; and he knew not ought he had, save the bread which he did eat. And Joseph was a goodly person, and well favoured.

⁷And it came to pass after these things, that his master's wife cast her eyes upon Joseph; and she said, Lie with me.

⁸But he refused, and said unto his master's wife, Behold, my master wotteth not what is with me in the house, and he hath committed all that he hath to my hand;

⁹There is none greater in this house than I; neither hath he kept back anything from me but thee, because thou art his wife: how then can I do this great wickedness, and sin against God?

¹⁰And it came to pass, as she spoke to Joseph day by day, that he hearkened not unto her, to lie by her, or to be with her.

¹¹ And it came to pass about this time, that Joseph went into the house to do his business; and there was none of the men of the house there within.

¹² And she caught him by his garment, saying, lie with me: and he left his garment in her hand, and fled, and got him out.

¹³ And it came to pass, when she saw that he had left his garment in her hand, and was fled forth,

¹⁴ That she called unto the men of her house, and spoke unto them, saying, See, he hath brought in a Hebrew unto us to mock us; he came in unto me to lie with me, and I cried with a loud voice:

¹⁵ And it came to pass, when he heard that I lifted up my voice and cried, that he left his garment with me, and fled, and got him out.

¹⁶ And she laid up his garment by her, until his lord came home.

¹⁷ And she spoke unto him according to these words, saying, The Hebrew servant, which thou hast brought unto us, came in unto me to mock me:

¹⁸ And it came to pass, as I lifted up my voice and cried, that he left his garment with me, and fled out.

¹⁹ And it came to pass, when his master heard the words of his wife, which she spoke unto him, saying, after this manner did thy servant to me; that his wrath was kindled.

²⁰ And Joseph's master took him, and put him into the prison, a place where the king's prisoners were bound: and he was there in the prison.

²¹ But the Lord was with Joseph, and shewed him mercy, and gave him favour in the sight of the keeper of the prison.

²² And the keeper of the prison committed to Joseph's hand all the prisoners that were in the prison; and whatsoever they did there, he was the doer of it.

²³ The keeper of the prison looked not to anything that was under his hand; because the Lord was with him, and that which he did, the Lord made it to prosper.

40 And it came to pass after these things, that the butler of the king of Egypt and his baker had offended their lord the king of Egypt.

² And Pharaoh was wroth against two of his officers, against the chief of the butlers, and against the chief of the bakers.

³ And he put them in ward in the house of the captain of the guard, into the prison, the place where Joseph was bound.

⁴ And the captain of the guard charged Joseph with them, and he served them: and they continued a season in ward.

⁵ And they dreamed a dream both of them, each man his dream in one night, each man according to the interpretation of his dream, the butler and the baker of the king of Egypt, which were bound in the prison.

⁶ And Joseph came in unto them in the morning, and looked upon them, and, behold, they were sad.

⁷ And he asked Pharaoh's officers that were with him in the ward of his lord's house, saying, wherefore look ye so sadly to day?

⁸ And they said unto him, we have dreamed a dream, and there is no interpreter of it. And Joseph said unto them, do not interpretations belong to God? tell me them, I pray you.

⁹ And the chief butler told his dream to Joseph, and said to him, In my dream, behold, a vine was before me;

¹⁰ And in the vine were three branches: and it was as though it budded, and her blossoms shot forth; and the clusters thereof brought forth ripe grapes:

¹¹ And Pharaoh's cup was in my hand: and I took the grapes, and pressed them into Pharaoh's cup, and I gave the cup into Pharaoh's hand.

¹² And Joseph said unto him, this is the interpretation of it: The three branches are three days:

¹³ Yet within three days shall Pharaoh lift up thine head, and restore thee unto thy place: and thou shalt deliver Pharaoh's cup into his hand, after the former manner when thou wast his butler.

¹⁴ But think on me when it shall be well with thee, and shew kindness, I pray thee, unto me, and make mention of me unto Pharaoh, and bring me out of this house:

¹⁵ For indeed I was stolen away out of the land of the Hebrews: and here also have I done nothing that they should put me into the dungeon.

¹⁶ When the chief baker saw that the interpretation was good, he said unto Joseph, I also was in my dream, and, behold, I had three white baskets on my head:

¹⁷ And in the uppermost basket there was of all manner of bake meats for Pharaoh; and the birds did eat them out of the basket upon my head.

¹⁸ And Joseph answered and said, this is the interpretation thereof: The three baskets are three days:

¹⁹ Yet within three days shall Pharaoh lift up thy head from off thee, and shall hang thee on a tree; and the birds shall eat thy flesh from off thee.

²⁰ And it came to pass the third day, which was Pharaoh's birthday, that he made a feast unto all his servants: and he lifted up the head of the chief butler and of the chief baker among his servants.

²¹ And he restored the chief butler unto his butlership again; and he gave the cup into Pharaoh's hand:

²² But he hanged the chief baker: as Joseph had interpreted to them.

²³ Yet did not the chief butler remember Joseph, but forgot him.

41 And it came to pass at the end of two full years, that Pharaoh dreamed: and, behold, he stood by the river.

² And, behold, there came up out of the river seven well favoured kine and fatfleshed; and they fed in a meadow.

³ And, behold, seven other kine came up after them out of the river, ill favoured and leanfleshed; and stood by the other kine upon the brink of the river.

⁴ And the ill favoured and leanfleshed kine did eat up the seven well favoured and fat kine. So, Pharaoh awoke.

⁵ And he slept and dreamed the second time: and, behold, seven ears of corn came up upon one stalk, rank and good.

⁶ And, behold, seven thin ears and blasted with the east wind sprung up after them.

⁷ And the seven thin ears devoured the seven rank and full ears. And Pharaoh awoke, and, behold, it was a dream.

⁸ And it came to pass in the morning that his spirit was troubled; and he sent and called for all the magicians of Egypt, and all the wise men thereof: and Pharaoh told them his dream; but there was none that could interpret them unto Pharaoh.

⁹ Then spoke the chief butler unto Pharaoh, saying, I do remember my faults this day:

¹⁰ Pharaoh was wroth with his servants, and put me in ward in the captain of the guard's house, both me and the chief baker:

¹¹ And we dreamed a dream in one night, I and he; we dreamed each man according to the interpretation of his dream.

¹² And there was there with us a young man, a Hebrew, servant to the captain of the guard; and we told him, and he interpreted to us our dreams; to each man according to his dream he did interpret.

¹³ And it came to pass, as he interpreted to us, so it was; me he restored unto mine office, and him he hanged. 14 Then Pharaoh sent and called Joseph, and they brought him hastily out of the dungeon: and he shaved himself, and changed his raiment, and came in unto Pharaoh.

¹⁵ And Pharaoh said unto Joseph, I have dreamed a dream, and there is none that can interpret it: and I have heard say of thee, that thou canst understand a dream to interpret it.

¹⁶ And Joseph answered Pharaoh, saying, it is not in me: God shall give Pharaoh an answer of peace.

¹⁷ And Pharaoh said unto Joseph, in my dream, behold, I stood upon the bank of the river:

¹⁸ And, behold, there came up out of the river seven kine, fatfleshed and well favoured; and they fed in a meadow:

¹⁹ And, behold, seven other kine came up after them, poor and very ill favoured and leanfleshed, such as I never saw in all the land of Egypt for badness:

²⁰ And the lean and the ill-favoured kine did eat up the first seven fat kine:

²¹ And when they had eaten them up, it could not be known that they had eaten them; but they were still ill favoured, as at the beginning. So, I awoke.

²² And I saw in my dream, and, behold, seven ears came up in one stalk, full and good:

²³ And, behold, seven ears, withered, thin, and blasted with the east wind, sprung up after them:

²⁴ And the thin ears devoured the seven good ears: and I told this unto the magicians; but there was none that could declare it to me.

²⁵ And Joseph said unto Pharaoh, the dream of Pharaoh is one: God hath shewed Pharaoh what he is about to do.

²⁶ The seven good kine are seven years; and the seven good ears are seven years: the dream is one.

²⁷ And the seven thin and ill-favoured kine that came up after them are seven years; and the seven empty ears blasted with the east wind shall be seven years of famine.

²⁸ This is the thing which I have spoken unto Pharaoh: What God is about to do he sheweth unto Pharaoh.

²⁹ Behold, there come seven years of great plenty throughout all the land of Egypt:

³⁰ And there shall arise after them seven years of famine; and all the plenty shall be forgotten in the land of Egypt; and the famine shall consume the land;

³¹ And the plenty shall not be known in the land by reason of that famine following; for it shall be very grievous.

³² And for that the dream was doubled unto Pharaoh twice; it is because the thing is established by God, and God will shortly bring it to pass.

³³ Now therefore let Pharaoh look out a man discreet and wise, and set him over the land of Egypt.

³⁴ Let Pharaoh do this, and let him appoint officers over the land, and take up the fifth part of the land of Egypt in the seven plenteous years.

³⁵ And let them gather all the food of those good years that come, and lay up corn under the hand of Pharaoh, and let them keep food in the cities.

³⁶ And that food shall be for store to the land against the seven years of famine, which shall be in the land of Egypt; that the land perishes not through the famine.

³⁷ And the thing was good in the eyes of Pharaoh, and in the eyes of all his servants.

³⁸ And Pharaoh said unto his servants, can we find such a one as this is, a man in whom the Spirit of God is? 39 And Pharaoh said unto Joseph, Forasmuch as God hath shewed thee all this, there is none so discreet and wise as thou art:

⁴⁰ Thou shalt be over my house, and according unto thy word shall all my people be ruled: only in the throne will I be greater than thou.

⁴¹ And Pharaoh said unto Joseph, See, I have set thee over all the land of Egypt.

⁴² And Pharaoh took off his ring from his hand, and put it upon Joseph's hand, and arrayed him in vestures of fine linen, and put a gold chain about his neck;

⁴³ And he made him to ride in the second chariot which he had; and they cried before him, Bow the knee: and he made him ruler over all the land of Egypt.

⁴⁴ And Pharaoh said unto Joseph, I am Pharaoh, and without thee shall no man lift up his hand or foot in all the land of Egypt.

⁴⁵ And Pharaoh called Joseph's name Zaphnathpaaneah; and he gave him to wife Asenath the daughter of Potipherah priest of On. And Joseph went out over all the land of Egypt.

⁴⁶ And Joseph was thirty years old when he stood before Pharaoh king of Egypt. And Joseph went out from the presence of Pharaoh, and went throughout all the land of Egypt.

⁴⁷ And in the seven plenteous years the earth brought forth by handfuls.

⁴⁸ And he gathered up all the food of the seven years, which were in the land of Egypt, and laid up the food in the cities: the food of the field, which was round about every city, laid he up in the same.

⁴⁹ And Joseph gathered corn as the sand of the sea, very much, until he left numbering; for it was without number.

⁵⁰ And unto Joseph were born two sons before the years of famine came, which Asenath the daughter of Potipherah priest of on bare unto him.

⁵¹ And Joseph called the name of the firstborn Manasseh: For God, said he, hath made me forget all my toil, and all my father's house.

⁵² And the name of the second called the Ephraim: For God hath caused me to be fruitful in the land of my affliction.

⁵³ And the seven years of plenteousness, that was in the land of Egypt, were ended.

⁵⁴ And the seven years of dearth began to come, according as Joseph had said: and the dearth was in all lands; but in all the land of Egypt there was bread.

⁵⁵ And when all the land of Egypt was famished, the people cried to Pharaoh for bread: and Pharaoh said unto all the Egyptians, Go unto Joseph; what he saith to you, do.

⁵⁶ And the famine was over all the face of the earth: and Joseph opened all the storehouses, and sold unto the Egyptians; and the famine waxed sore in the land of Egypt.

⁵⁷ And all countries came into Egypt to Joseph for to buy corn; because that the famine was so sore in all lands.

SEEK AND FIND BY WORDS

```
C I Y Z L O V W E L L F A V O U R E D Y O F I N E U L L R O D
A A I F A L O D E V E R T H I N G D I R H A V E B E L O N G S
R R L A P P V E O Q S A P E S H O A E T B C L L A Q C U H X T
L R L T P C H Y O G U I H S B O B L J B I I V N Y Z H O B Y O
A A I H O A P N F P A N O L F M T Z O E N S F E T L A A R B T
Y Y B E I R O M A M K T L O Z U E O S S T L Y Y O R I I D N H
O E E R N L P Z M T I E Y R B A N X E T E O E G A T N U T C E
C D R Y T T S A I A H R E D B A I C P S R Z T H O G X O G O A
A Z N O U G E L N L M P A S T A K K H O P E P C Q Y O U O M L
P E I F P A G L E L V R A X S A C E E M R A R E M Y A L O E M
T V C T O V Y T H A N E K A U T D K R E E S E T W O N L D R I
A A E A S O P R O Z Q T V T N F A T H E T T R I U N E A D E G
I L O N K E T E F G A A L E L E H O L Y C D E V O U R E D L H
N S U E O T I T L O G T F O P R A S I R Q S Z U F A L L S U T
O Y E K O H A S Q L A I D T A A T H H Y E A R S F G L A A R Y
F Y H G B E N A Z D W O V E R S E E R K N H Z I I H M E V E A
T E E A Y W X M Q Z W N H O T U Y O F D W E S N C N N H A D N
H S A K I P R I S O N S N A I C I G A M I A E T E A S T Q N D
E T N W D H T S A H S I F A S M L B S O C V N N R T X C Z W N
G B N A R E B M E M E R C Q I O A U E R K E I A S H D R T O O
U E O N A C A N D A C E U K G R R T N N E L T T H E E I B H O
A L T E F A T F L E S H E D H A R L A I D H H O L Y A D C S N
R O N K F A T L E G G S W I T I Y L T N N S P I R I T R T A E
D N I A B A R E S E R I E S S M L R H G E D O O F S H E L C E
I G U U R A H P I T O P H G W E X E T T S E R I Q A E A I C L
O S Q R A G S T O B L E C S A N U N F D S E F P R W S M E O S
W E T H Y N H A N E D Q R A E T E J I N T T S E R I E S O R E
E C W H O I C H N A M A E R N M H S F I H F H E A S T C C S T
E R S S Z X J T J T E O O G R K C A S W T G E C A M E O T D O
V T R I C H Y E S H A N D A M R H N Z I M S H A V E D A O I T
E S J C O M M I T T E D G T E T H E H O L Y N E N I L I T N H
R L A N D T O Y O U F A T E H E R C T H I R T Y M K O C K G E
Y T H I N P R O S P E R T H A T S E V E N O S A S E C I W T T
```

1. APPOINT
2. ARRAYED
3. ASENATH
4. BAKER
5. BARE
6. BELONG
7. BUTLER
8. CAPTAIN OF THE GUARD
9. CHAIN
10. COMMITTED
11. CORN
12. DEVOURED
13. DISCREET
14. DREAMS
15. EARS
16. EAST
17. EGYPT
18. EGYPTIAN
19. FAMINE
20. FAT FLESHED
21. FIFTH
22. FINE
23. FOOD
24. FOOT
25. GARMENT
26. GOD
27. GOLD
28. GOOD
29. ILL
30. INTERPRET
31. INTERPRETATIONS
32. JOSEPH
33. KINE
34. LAND
35. LEAN
36. LEAN FLESHED
37. LINEN
38. LORD
39. MAGICIANS
40. MASTER
41. MORNING
42. OFFICERS
43. OVERSEER
44. PART
45. PHARAOH
46. PLENTY
47. POTIPHAR
48. PRISON
49. PROSPER
50. RAIMENT
51. REMEMBER
52. RING
53. RULER
54. SEE
55. SEVEN
56. SHAVED
57. SHOWN
58. SIN
59. SLAVE
60. SONS
61. STALK
62. THIRTY
63. TWICE
64. TWO
65. WELL FAVOURED
66. WICKEDNESS
67. YEARS
68. YEARS
69. ZAPHNATHPAANEAH

FEELINGS

(In order to learn about each person's feelings, you must first unscramble the words then place them in the space next to the same number)

1. FHECI TLUBER DNA KRBAE
2. SPHJOE
3. PRPASIHOT EWFI
4. ARHPPTIO
5. GDO
6. HAPHROA
7. HFECI RBAEK
8. IHFEC BERLUT

_____ He caused Joseph to have favour with all men and He protected Joseph.

_____ They were very upset because they were put in prison.

_____ He was a slave and he prayed to God for help and guidance and he believed God would help him.

_____ She wanted Joseph so badly that she lied on him.

_____ He was so happy with Joseph that he made him overseer of his house.

_____ He was very upset because no one could tell him what the dream was about that he had dreamed.

_____ The Pharaoh had him hanged.

_____ He was very happy to go back to serving the Pharaoh.

SCRAMBLE / UNSCRAMBLE

FHECI TLUBER DNA KRBAE

_____

SPHOJE

_____

PRPASIHOT EWFI

_____

ARHPTIOP

_____

GDO

_____

HARHPOA

_____

HFECI RBAEK

_____

IHFEC BERLUT

_____

ORDER OF EVENTS

(MUST PUT EACH NUMBER IN THE CORRECT
ORDER IN WHICH THE EVENT TOOK PLACE)

_____ a. JOSEPH IS THROWN INTO PRISON

_____ b. POTIPHAR BUYS JOSEPH AS A SLAVE

_____ c. PHARAOH HANGED THE CHIEF BAKER

_____ d. JOSPEH GATHERED CORN AS THE SAND
OF THE SEA

_____ e. POTIPHAR WIFE LIED ON JOSEPH

_____ f. JOSEPH ANSWERED PHARAOH, SAYING, IT
IS NOT IN ME: GOD SHALL GIVE PHARAOH
AN ANSWER OF PEACE

_____ g. AND UNTO JOSEPH WERE BORN TWO
SONS BEFORE THE YEARS OF FAMINE CAME

_____ h. GOD GAVE JOSEPH THE
INTERPRETATIONS OF BOTH THE CHIEF
BUTLER AND THE CHIEF BAKER DREAMS

_____ i. PHARAOH TOLD HIS DREAM TO ALL THE
MAGICIANS OF EGYPT, AND ALL THE WISE
MEN THEREOF: BUT THERE WAS NONE
THAT COULD INTREPRET THEM.

_____ j. AND THERE WAS NONE OF THE MEN OF
THE HOUSE THERE WITHIN.

_____ k. AND THE LORD MADE ALL THAT JOSEPH
DID TO PROSPER IN HIS HAND.

_____ l. THERE SHALL COME SEVEN YEARS OF
PLENTY AND AFTER THAT SHALL ARISE
SEVEN YEARS OF FAMINE.

_____ m. JOSPEH WAS THIRTY YEARS OLD WHEN HE
STOOD BEFORE PHARAOH KING OF EGYPT.

_____ n. THE CHIEF BUTLER REMEMBER HIS
FAULTS PHARAOH ABOUT JOSEPH
INTERPRETING HIS BAKER'S DREAMS.

WHO ARE THEY

(You must draw a straight line from each noun, to the
answer that explains that particular noun.)

ZAPHNATHPAANEAH

a. She became Joseph wife.

GOD

b. The Pharaoh had these men put in prison.

POTIPHAR'S WIFE

c. God gave him the interpretation of dreams.

MANASSEH AND
EPHRAIM

d. Joseph ruled in second command under this man.

JOSEPH

e. He finally remembered Joseph in prison and told the Pharaoh about Joseph.

POTIPHAR

f. She lied on and about Joseph to the men in the house and to her husband.

ASENATH

g. Joseph prayed to him and he caused Joseph to prosper and to find favour wherever he went.

CHIEF BAKER AND
CHIEF BUTLER

h. He made Joseph overseer over his house.

PHARAOH

i. The Pharaoh changed Joseph's name to this.

CHIEF BUTLER

j. They are the names of the two sons born to Joseph in Egypt.

```
G E N E S I S 4 0 2 0 3 3 0 G G 4 1 1 4 S I S E N E G
E E S 1 4 S I S N E 3 3 G L E E 8 3 G S I 4 6 4 5 E E
N G N G E N E S I S I 7 E 4 N N 4 E N E S 5 9 7 N G N
E E N E 4 2 1 3 2 4 G 8 N 4 E E 9 S 7 I 4 G 3 E S E E
S S I 0 S E N E S S E 4 E 1 S I 0 I 0 3 E S S 4 I N S
I 4 7 8 5 I 3 I 3 I N 5 S S I S 9 S 5 N I I I I S 7 I
S G E N E O S 6 9 S E 4 I I I S 4 8 4 E S S 4 S 3 G I S
I E N E G E 7 4 I S 8 3 S S 3 0 4 S I 4 7 I E I E 4 3
4 N 2 4 N 9 5 6 1 3 S 2 4 E 9 3 3 N 0 8 I 2 N G N S 9
3 S 3 E 8 8 3 2 1 5 I I 1 N 2 0 E I 9 2 2 3 E E E I 2
9 I G E N E G 4 8 S 2 0 2 E 1 G 2 0 0 7 4 5 G N S S 3
G E N E S I S 7 4 I 3 0 5 G E N E S I S G E N E I E G
E E N 5 4 I 0 8 G E N E S I S 4 1 4 9 S E N E G S N E
S I N G S S I S E N E G E N E S I S 3 9 1 9 3 E G E N
0 9 3 E I 4 S I S N E G E N S G E N E S I S 4 N 9 G E
S 1 N 4 S I S E N N E G E I E 8 S I S E N E G E 0 E S
I E 1 G 9 I E G E S I S S N 4 3 S I S E N E G S 4 N I
G 8 E I N N S S S G E N E S I S 4 1 I 2 0 8 E I I E 2
S 9 8 E S I I 4 E G S S G E N E S S I 3 9 G N S S S 1
7 6 5 I S S G N I S I G E S G E N E 1 7 N E E 4 5 I 9
7 3 S E 4 E E N I S 4 8 E I S I S 4 G E I N S 1 N S 3
6 4 N 1 N S N E 4 7 I S N S 3 3 S 5 S G S S I 4 E 3 S
4 E 1 E I S E 1 3 9 1 7 0 4 S I S E N E G I S 6 6 9 I
G 3 S S I G 1 G E 1 7 8 6 7 S E G S E N S S 4 7 4 6 S
6 I 4 S E 3 N E S I 3 4 8 E E N S I N E G 1 8 G S E S
S 1 G N 3 S I S 4 9 G E N E S I S 3 9 2 0 E S S I G N
9 E E 4 8 8 7 4 3 2 I E I 2 3 8 4 G E N E S I N S E E
G E N E S I S 4 1 8 G E N S I S G 2 0 4 S I S E N E G
```

1. What verse tells you that the Lord was with Joseph and showed Joseph mercy, and gave Joseph favour in the sight of the keeper of the prison?
2. Where does it say that the chief baker saw that the interpretation was good so he told his dream to Joseph?
3. What verse says that the Pharaoh's spirit was troubled and he sent for all the magicians of Egypt?
4. What verse tells you that the keeper of the prison looked not to anything that was under Joseph's hand?
5. This verse says that the chief butler tells of the hanging of the chief baker as Joseph had interpreted.
6. Where does it say that Pharaoh was wroth against his two officers, the chief butler and the chief baker?
7. Where does it say that Potiphar bought Joseph from the hands of the Ishmeelites?
8. Which verse says that they brought Joseph out of the dungeon hastily?
9. In what verse does the chief butler says he remember his faults today?
10. What verse does the chief butler tell the Pharaoh the interpretation that Joseph gave him?
11. Can you find the verse that Joseph was thirty years old when he stood before Pharaoh?
12. In this verse Joseph asks the Pharaoh's officers wherefore look ye so sadly today?
13. This is where Pharaoh asks can we find a man in whom the Spirit of God is?
14. What verse says that Potiphar left all that he had in Joseph's hand?
15. Here the chief butler tells Pharaoh that a young Hebrew interpreted their dreams?

16. Where does it tell you that Joseph tells Pharaoh that God has showed him what He is about to do?

17. This is the verse that Potiphar's wife caught Joseph by his garment and Joseph left the garment in her hand and fled.

18. Where does it tell you that on the third day it was Pharaoh's birthday and that he made a feast for his servants?

19. What verse lets you know that it was Joseph's master that put him into prison?

20. Joseph tells the chief butler that the three branches are three days?

21. Here Joseph tells the Pharaoh to look for a man discreet and wise and to set him over the land of Egypt.

22. Which verse says that Joseph left off numbering the corn for it was without number?

23. Find where Joseph tells Pharaoh that the plenty will be forgotten, and the famine shall consume the land?

24. What verse did Joseph say, For God hath caused me to be fruitful in the land of my affliction?

1. _____	9. _____	17. _____
2. _____	10. _____	18. _____
3. _____	11. _____	19. _____
4. _____	12. _____	20. _____
5. _____	13. _____	21. _____
6. _____	14. _____	22. _____
7. _____	15. _____	23. _____
8. _____	16. _____	24. _____

CONNECT THE DOTS

(SEE JOSEPH IN THE MIDST OF THE COUNTLESS CORN)

CROSSWORD PUZZLE

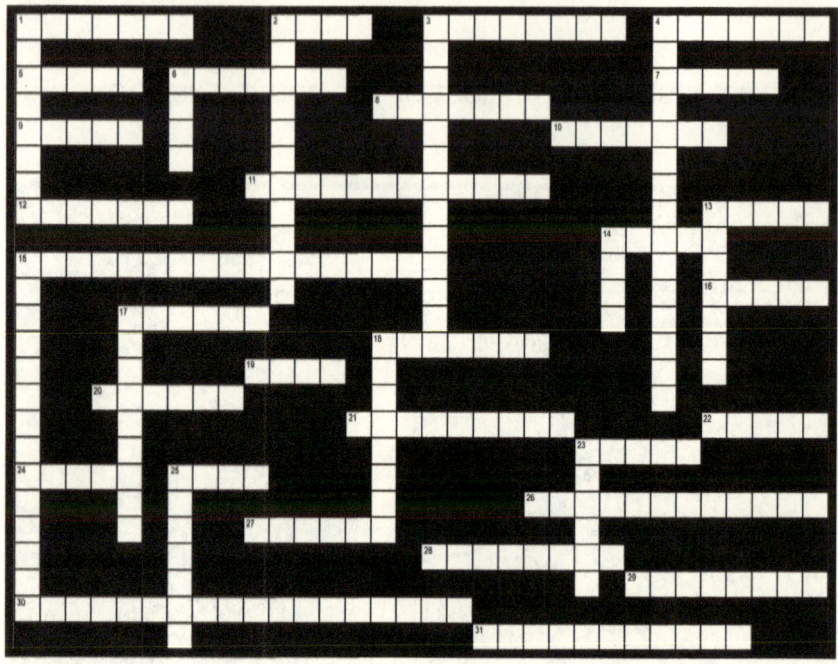

ACROSS

1. Joseph left this that belonged to him, in his master's wife hand.
2. Because the _____ was with Joseph, and that which he did the _____ made it to prosper.
3. He brought Joseph when Joseph was brought down to Egypt.
4. She is who Pharaoh gave to Joseph to wife.
5. The dream was doubled unto Pharaoh _____, it is because the thing is established by God.
6. Joseph was a _____ to the captain of the guard.
7. Joseph was put in a _____ where the king's prisoners were bound.
8. They brought Joseph hastily out of this place.
9. Joseph was sold in this place and brought by an officer of Pharaoh.

CROSSWORD PUZZLE

(Continued)

10. The Pharaoh sent and called Joseph and they brought him _____ out of the dungeon.
11. The thin fleshed kine devoured the _____ and fat kine.
12. The past tense of dream.
13. Pharaoh put a gold _____ about Joseph neck.
14. They were to take up a _____ part of the land of Egypt in the seven plenteous years.
15. He looked not to anything that was under Joseph's hand.
16. In the Pharaoh's dream he stood by this body of water.
17. Joseph a _____, was servant to the captain of the guard.
18. And it came to pass after these things that Joseph's _____ wife cast her eyes upon him.
19. Joseph gathered up all the _____ of the seven years, which were in the land of Egypt.
20. Potiphar had Joseph placed in here because of what his wife said about Joseph.
21. Pharaoh sent and called for all the _____ of Egypt.
22. The Lord shewed this to Joseph and gave him favour in the sight of the keeper of the prison.
23. The seven ears of corn came up on one of these.
24. This is the years of dearth began to come according as Joseph had said.
25. Asenath _____ Joseph two sons.
26. Joseph was a _____ and well favoured.
27. God gave the Pharaoh the interpretation of his dreams through this man.
28. And, behold, seven ears, _____, thin.
29. The seven thin ears _____ the rank and full ears.
30. There will be seven years of plenty throughout Egypt followed by _____ _____
31. He told the Pharaoh that Joseph had interpreted their dreams.

CROSSWORD PUZZLE

(Continued)

DOWN

1. He told the Pharaoh that Joseph had interpreted their dreams.
2. Behold seven other kine came up after them, poor and very ill favoured and _____, such as I never saw in the land of Egypt for badness.
3. The seven years of _____ that was in the land of Egypt, were ended.
4. Let Pharaoh do this, and let him _____ _____ over the land.
6. The famine was waxed _____ in the land.
13. The Pharaoh made Joseph to ride in the second _____ which he had.
14. Joseph _____ from Potiphar's wife and got him out.
15. Joseph's master took him and put him into the prison, a place where the _____ _____ were bound.
17. Joseph _____ not unto his master's wife
18. Joseph named him this because he said God hath made me forget all my toil and all my father's house.
23. Joseph said for indeed I was _____ away out of the land of the Hebrews.
25. The seven ears, withered, thin and _____ with the east wind, sprung up after them.

UNSCRAMBLE THE WORDS

1. GETPY   _ _ _ _ _
2. RLDO   _ _ _ _
3. ERVEOERS   _ _ _ _ _ _ _ _
4. SOPEJH   _ _ _ _ _ _
5. THRIAPOP   _ _ _ _ _ _ _ _
6. SRRPOPE   _ _ _ _ _ _ _
7. GDO   _ _ _
8. EIFW   _ _ _ _
9. ROHPAAH   _ _ _ _ _ _ _
10. DFVEORUA   _ _ _ _ _ _ _ _
11. GACIMASIN   _ _ _ _ _ _ _ _
12. MADRES   _ _ _ _ _ _
13. INSRPO   _ _ _ _ _ _
14. KRBEA   _ _ _ _ _
15. ULREBT   _ _ _ _ _ _
16. VRRIE   _ _ _ _ _
17. EPRTIDEETNR   _ _ _ _ _ _ _ _ _ _
18. RYASE   _ _ _ _ _
19. SENVE   _ _ _ _ _
20. SAHESMAN   _ _ _ _ _ _ _ _
21. MEPARHI   _ _ _ _ _ _ _
22. NATSEHA   _ _ _ _ _ _ _

DEFINITIONS

1. ARRAY - To dress or decorate in finery; adorn.
2. BAKER – The one who cooks bake goods (such as breads, cakes)
3. BUTLER – The head male servant of a house hold. (In this case the one who served the Pharaoh and tasted everything before he gave it to the Pharaoh)
4. CHIEF – one of the highest ranks or authority; leader.
5. DEVOURED – To eat up really fast.
6. DISCREET – Having or displaying caution and self- restraint: prudent.
7. DREAMS – A vision that occurs in sleep; what appears to you while you're resting at night.
8. FAMINE – A drastic, wide-ranging food shortage
9. GOD – The Creator of the Heavens and Earth, everything that is and was to come; everything that dwells in the Earth. He is the Creator of mankind; He created man from the dust of the Earth and He breathed into man's nostrils, the breath of life and man became a living soul; and no one can breathe without HIM. He is the Creator of every kind of fish, every bird, every animal and everything that walketh or creepeth upon, above or beneath the Earth and everything that lives in the waters. In which He caused everything and everyone to produce after its own kind. He created every fruit and vegetable and He put seeds in them to produce after its own kind. He created all the water and all the land and everything in it, below it or above it. Without Him there was nothing that was made in the Heaven or the Earth.
10. INTERPRETATE – To explain a mystery or something that another doesn't understand. To make it understood plainly.
11. INTREPRETATIONS – To be interpreted; to be explained.
12. JOSEPH – He is the eleventh son of Jacob (whose name was changed to Israel), He was placed in a well by his brothers. Then later with a change of heart Joseph was taken out of the well and sold into slavery by his own brothers to the Ishmeelites. He was later sold in Egypt to Potiphar. He was falsely accused and put into prison. He became the second in command to the Pharaoh. Thru him GOD saved a nation (Israel), and the world from famine.
13. KINE- a specific type.

14. LEAN FLESHED – bad looking, not desirable, and thin.
15. MAGICIANS – They were expected to be experts, in handling the daily ritual books of black magic; to know something about everything. To be able to interpret dreams; especially one of the Pharaoh.
16. MASTER – One with control, or authority over another or others.
17. MERCHANT – One who buys, trades, and sells goods for money; to make a living.
18. PHARAOH – He was the ruler over all of Egypt. He put his chief butler and chief baker in prison. He had a dream that not one person out of all the magicians and neither any of all the wise men of Egypt could interpret it for him. He was given the interpretation of his dream by God. God revealed the interpretation of his dream to Joseph. He made Joseph second in command over all of Egypt. He gave Joseph the name Zaphnathpaaneah.
19. PLENTY –Abundance; more than enough. So much you can't even count it.
20. POTIPHAR – He was an officer of Pharaoh. He was the Egyptian who bought Joseph from the Ishmeelites. When he saw that Joseph's God favoured and caused everything that he did to prosper; he made Joseph overseer of and over his house.
21. PRISON – A place of confinement for one who is accused of some kind of wrong doing; convicted persons.
22. RAIMENT – Clothing, garment, apparel; what you wear to cover up your body.
23. RULER – One who rules; one in authority. He or she tells others what to do and how to do it.
24. SHAVED – To remove hair (such as a beard) with a razor.
25. SIN – To do something against God or mankind. The act of breaking a mortal law given by God or man.
26. SLAVE – A person who is brought with money or traded in lieu of money. One who is bound to servitude; a person who is the property of another person, or household. One who is no longer free to do as he wishes.
27. WELL FAVOURED – Very pleasing to the eyes; good and fine looking.

SEEK AND FIND

(ANSWER KEY)

FEELINGS
(ANSWER KEY)

5

1

2

3

4

6

7

8

UNSCRAMBLES

1.   Chief Butler and Baker

2.   Joseph

3.   Potiphar's wife

4.   Potiphar

5.   GOD

6.   Pharaoh

7.   Chief Baker

8.   Chief Butler

ORDER OF EVENTS

(ANSWER KEY)

1. B
2. K
3. J
4. E
5. A
6. H
7. C
8. I
9. N
10. F
11. L
12. M
13. D
14. G

WHO ARE THEY?
(ANSWER KEY)

1. I
2. G
3. F
4. J
5. C
6. H
7. A
8. B
9. D
10.E

SEEK AND FIND BY VERSE

(ANSWER KEY)

1.	Genesis 39:21	13.	Genesis 41:38
2.	Genesis 40:16	14.	Genesis 39:6
3.	Genesis 41:8	15.	Genesis 41:12
4.	Genesis 39:23	16.	Genesis 41:25
5.	Genesis 41:13	17.	Genesis 39:12
6.	Genesis 40:2	18.	Genesis 40:20
7.	Genesis 39:1	19.	Genesis 39:20
8.	Genesis 41:14	20.	Genesis 40:12
9.	Genesis 41:9	21.	Genesis 41:33
10.	Genesis 41:13	22.	Genesis 41: 49
11.	Genesis 41:46	23.	Genesis 41:30
12.	Genesis 40:7	24.	Genesis 41:52

CONNECT THE DOTS
(ANSWER KEY)

CROSSWORD PUZZLE

(ANSWER KEY)

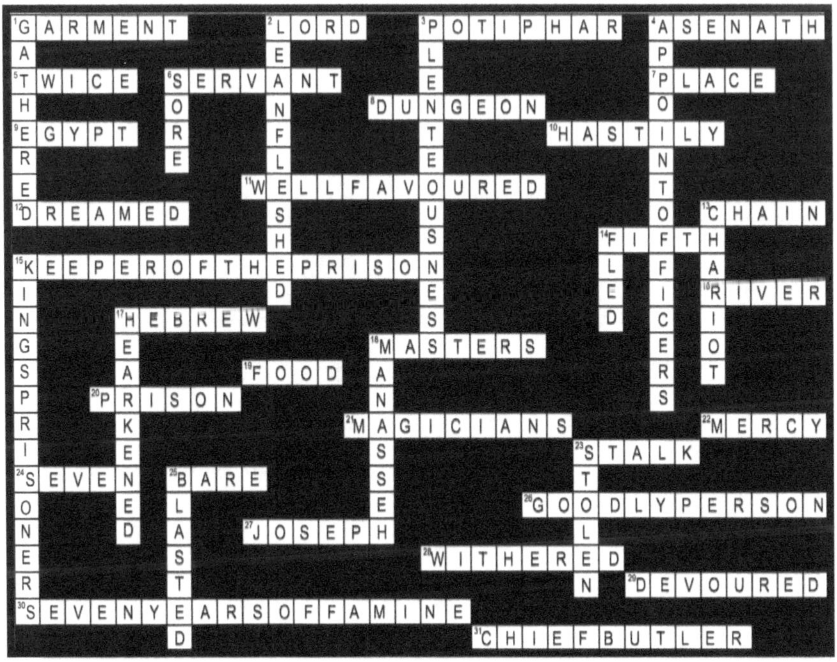
1 GARMENT
2 LORD
3 POTIPHAR
4 ASENATH
5 TWICE
6 SERVANT
7 PLACE
8 DUNGEON
9 EGYPT
10 HASTILY
11 WELLFAVOURED
12 DREAMED
13 CHAIN
14 FIFTH
15 KEEPEROFTHEPRISON
16 RIVER
17 HEBREW
18 MASTERS
19 FOOD
20 PRISON
21 MAGICIANS
22 MERCY
23 STALK
24 SEVEN
25 BARE
26 GOODLYPERSON
27 JOSEPH
28 WITHERED
29 DEVOURED
30 SEVENYEARSOFFAMINE
31 CHIEFBUTLER
GATHERED
LEANFLESHED
PLENTEOUSNESS
APPOINTOFFICERS
SORE
CHARIOT
FLED
KINGSPRISONER
HEARKENED
MANASSEH
STOLEN
BLASTED

CROSSWORD PUZZLE

(Continued)

ACROSS

1. Garment
2. Lord
3. Potiphar
4. Asenath
5. Twice
6. Servant
7. Place
8. Dungeon
9. Egypt
10. Hastily
11. Well favoured
12. Dreamed
13. Chain
14. Fifth
15. Keeper of the prison
16. River
17. Hebrew
18. Master's
19. Food
20. Prison
21. Magicians
22. Mercy
23. Stalk
24. Seven
25. Bare
26. Goodly person
27. Joseph
28. Withered
29. Devoured
30. Seven years of famine
31. Chief butler

DOWN

1. Gathered
2. Lean fleshed
3. Plenteousness
4. Appoint Officers
5. Sore
6. Chariot
7. Fled
8. Kings prisoners
9. Hearkened
10. Manasseh
11. Stolen
12. Blasted

UNSCRAMBLE THE WORDS
(ANSWER KEY)

1. EGYPT
2. LORD
3. OVERSEER
4. JOSEPH
5. POTIPHAR
6. PROSPER
7. GOD
8. WIFE
9. PHARAOH
10. FAVOURED
11. MAGICIANS
12. DREAMS
13. PRISON
14. BAKER
15. BUTLER
16. RIVER
17. INTERPRETED
18. YEARS
19. SEVEN
20. MANASSEH
21. EPHRAIM
22. ASENATH

SALVATION

Romans 10:9-10

That if thou shalt confess with thy mouth the Lord Jesus, and shalt believe in thine heart that God hath raised him from the dead, thou shalt be saved. 10 For with the heart man believeth unto righteousness; and with the mouth confession is made unto salvation.

John 1:10-12

He was in the world, and the world was made by him, and the world knew him not. He came unto his own, and his own received him not. 12 But as many as received him, to them gave he power to become the sons of God, even to them that believe on his name:

PRAYER OF SALVATION

Dear God, You said if I would believe with all my heart that Jesus died for my sins and rose from the dead that I would be saved. So now in the name of Jesus Christ, I ask you to wash me in His precious blood. I receive, this day, Jesus Christ as my Lord and Savior and I thank you for saving me.

If you repeated this prayer and meant it from your heart, you are now saved. Welcome to the family of God!

www.ingramcontent.com/pod-product-compliance
Lightning Source LLC
Chambersburg PA
CBHW031240120626
46545CB00003B/1211